Rome travel guide

The perfect travel guide for an un-forgettable stay in Rome

including insider tips and money-saving advice

Roman Hünsche

CONTENTS

What you can expect in this book

Rome. What do you associate with this city? - Do you think Rome is the Eternal City? The city that you feel has always been there? The one that fascinated and accompanied you in your Latin lessons?

Is Rome for you the city where the ancient Romans strolled across the Roman Forum and gladiators fought fierce battles in the Colosseum? Would you like to get to know the city where the great emperors such as Caesar or Augustus ruled and do you dream of one day walking in the footsteps of Romulus and Remus, the founding fathers of Rome?

Or do you think: Rome? - That's the Holy City where the Pope resides and which for a long time has regularly attracted pilgrims and made them rave about it, so that you always have the feeling of missing out on something 'divine' and 'healing' if you've never been there?

Thomas Mann once said: 'See Venice and die'. But let's be honest, shouldn't he have said 'See Rome and die'? Because there's something about this city that you never forget once you've been there.

Or perhaps you are passionate about architecture and long to explore St. Peter's Basilica, Castel Sant'Angelo or the Pantheon up close - or are you an art lover and would like to marvel at the original works of Raphael, Michelangelo or Caravaggio? All this is possible in Italy's great, time-honored and majestic capital, which lies on the beautiful Tiber River.

But even if you want to get to know Rome from its lively, modern and youthful-fresh side, you are guaranteed to get your money's worth and plan your next stay in this versatile metropolis before you leave - usually far too early.

Imagine what it would be like to stroll through the typical narrow streets of an Italian town in bright sunshine and completely forget that you are in a big city?

But would you also like to enjoy Rome's bustling shopping streets and perhaps even spend a small fortune on the famous 'Chic & Shock Street', Via Condotti? Is the city perhaps even the epitome of a hip fashion metropolis for you, with which you associate elegant, high-quality clothing 'Made in Italy'? Then you should definitely not miss out on Rome!

If your desire to travel has now been awakened, you will be able to read lots of exciting information about the history of Rome in this book, but of course you will also find numerous tips on how to make your trip to the Eternal City varied, relaxing and as cost-effective as possible.
You can also look forward to some real insider tips and useful advice on topics such as travel, accommodation, food and drink and proper Italian 'netiquette'. And of course the 'shopaholics' among you won't miss out either!

I hope you enjoy reading this book and that Rome will soon be able to welcome you for an unforgettable stay.

Well then, andiamo! Let's get started!

The birth of Rome

As you probably already know, Rome is a very old city. However, it has by no means always been a large metropolis.

Early or ancient Rome developed between 1000 and 800 BC from the first individual small villages that were located on hills around what is now the city. These world-famous seven hills of Rome bear the names Aventine, Caelius, Esquiline, Capitoline, Palatine, Quirinal and Viminal and formed a rather inconspicuous and rather unattractive, marshy area east of the Tiber, which, however, had a decisive advantage: it was located on important trade routes. It was also this aspect that turned the cluster of small villages into a fortified city by the middle of the 8th century BC, albeit a manageable one, and into the strategic center of the later Roman Empire (Latin 'Imperium Romanum').

This period of Etruscan rule also saw two important construction projects for the city: Firstly, a sophisticated sewer system, the 'Cloaca Maxima', was built, which made the swampy area on which early Rome stood usable. At the same time, a kind of central square was created in the city, which would one day become the Roman Forum we know today.

The Forum Romanum, which we can translate as the Roman marketplace, was the center of all religious, cultural, political and economic life in ancient Rome and is today one of the most important excavation sites of this period.
Parallel to this historical story of Rome's development, there is also a founding myth which states that Rome was founded by Romulus on April 21, 753 BC. You are no doubt familiar with the well-known mnemonic: 'Seven-five-three: Rome crawled out of the egg'.

According to legend, the twin brothers Romulus and Remus were the children of the god of war

Mars and the priestess Rhea Silvia. As their mother was unable to raise them as a priestess and was not allowed to do so anyway, the two children were abandoned in a wicker basket on the Tiber and eventually found and taken in by a she-wolf on its banks.

You are therefore probably familiar with the depiction of a she-wolf suckling two children. Later, the two brothers clashed as grown men in a dispute over the city walls of Rome and Romulus killed Remus in the course of this dispute.

Explore ancient Rome

If you would like to find traces of early Rome in the present day, you can of course start by admiring many of the ancient buildings (see Chapter 4) up close.

But you can also look for hidden signs of this ancient time.

The she-wolf suckling Romulus and Remus is once exhibited in the Capitoline Museums as a life-size bronze statue. She is a very important and popular symbol of Rome, as she stands for eternity (of the city/empire) and immortality. It is also often depicted on coins, medals or mosaics.

However, she also appears a second time in the city, standing on a column.

<u>Task 1</u>: Find the column with the 'Lupa Romana' in Rome and guess which of the seven hills of Rome you are now on!

If you explore the city on foot, you will also frequently see the abbreviation 'S. P. Q. R.' on many everyday objects such as manhole covers or garbage cans, as well as on a number of public facilities and souvenir stores and other places in Rome.

This abbreviation also originates from ancient Rome, as it was the national emblem of the time and the legions of the Roman Empire wore it on their standards. The abbreviation means 'Senatus Populusque Romanus' in Latin, which can be translated as 'Senate and People of Rome'.

<u>Task 2</u>: While strolling through Rome, look for the abbreviation 'S. P. Q. R.' and count how many times you can find it!

But what happened to Rome next? After the founding period, Rome was initially a kingdom ruled by Etruscan kings. You will certainly know the first great successor Romulus from the history books under the name Numa Pompilius. This kingdom lasted until around 500 BC and ended with the expulsion of the last Etruscan king, Tarquinius Superbus.

Rome then became a republic, characterized by struggles between the free but disenfranchised plebeians and the aristocratic patricians. At the same time, Rome continued to expand so that the surrounding areas were also annexed.

Incidentally, today there are three other well-known hills in the city of Rome, namely the Vaticano, the Gianicolo and the Pincio.

Nevertheless, from 390 BC the city was almost constantly threatened by attacks from other peoples, which is why the 'Servian Wall', a high and strong city wall, was finally built.

Other important structures from the time around 312 BC are the 'Aqueduct', which was a kind of above-ground water pipe, and the 'Via

Appia', which could be seen as an important long-distance and trade route and is now the longest museum in the world, as many historical buildings and tombs can be found along this road.

Rome then underwent further expansion, particularly from 264 to 146 BC, when it successfully fought against the North African Carthaginians. These wars are known as the 'Punic Wars'. Unfortunately, this was followed by a period of civil war and unrest after the popular tribunes and brothers Tiberius and Gaius Sempronius Gracchus were murdered and the dictator Gaius Iulius Caesar was also killed in 44 BC.

Before this, however, Caesar had tried to push through various reforms. He had been particularly successful in this through the famous 'triumvirate' (= alliance of three men) with Marcus Licinius Crassus and Gnaeus Pompeius Magnus.

In the meantime, Rome had reached a size that necessitated further expansion of the area and made the Forum Romanum too small, so Caesar began to build the 'Forum Iulium', the oldest of Rome's four imperial forums. This forum was finally completed by Caesar's successor Augustus in the 1st century BC.

At this time, the imperial age of Rome began and the city had already become a city of millions. Moreover, Rome was now also the center of the Roman Empire in geographical and political terms. It was above all Emperor Augustus who promoted the expansion of Rome and ensured that the city had many advanced amenities, such as a functioning sewage system.

These achievements were briefly set back by the fire of Rome in 64 BC under Emperor Nero, but the reign of the 'Flavian dynasty' began soon afterwards from 69 to 96 AD, which was characterized by extensive construction measures financed by the emperors.

During a visit to Rome, you will be able to recognize the Colosseum and, of course, the Imperial Forums from this period and the large thermal baths were also typical of this time, which are regarded as the high point of the Roman Empire.

A real competition arose at the time and many emperors were driven by the idea of having to outdo their respective predecessors and demonstrate their power with ever larger buildings. As a result, Rome continued to grow, so that in the 3rd century a new city wall, the 'Aurelian Wall', had to be built, as the city had long since exceeded the limits of the Servian Wall. The estimated population at the time was 1.2 million people.

However, as quickly as Rome had risen, it soon lost this exposed supremacy again. Many emperors preferred residences in other cities and Constantinople in particular became increasingly competitive in the 4th century.

In the 5th century, civil wars broke out again and Rome was plundered several times, once in 410 by Gothic mercenaries and most notably in 455 AD by the Vandals. Did you know that this is one of the origins of the saying 'Live like the Vandals'?

This already decimated the population of Rome again. A further rapid decline occurred from 429 AD, however, due to the fact that Rome had less and less control over North Africa and important grain supplies from there for the Roman citizens failed to materialize.

This marked the final end of the Western Roman Empire in 476 AD, but ancient life was initially continued under the rule of the Ostrogoths, although the population continued to decline and in 530 there were only 100,000 people left in Rome.

Only the subsequent Gothic Wars and the reconquest attempts by Emperor Justinian led to the dissolution of the senatorial class and the destruction of supplies and urban life from 537 AD.

The ensuing siege battles further reduced the population to a few tens of thousands and in 550 AD the last chariot races were held in the 'Circus Maximus'.

The Roman Forum also finally lost its importance for the city of Rome and the ancient monuments were left to decay. Rome was thus reduced to the status of a provincial city and only the papacy retained a remnant of importance for the city.

<u>Explore the emerging empire of Rome</u>

If you are now wondering where you can find traces of Rome's eventful and exciting heyday, there are plenty of opportunities to do so in the city, two of which you will find somewhat unusual suggestions here.

<u>Suggestion 1</u>: Take a bike tour on the 'Via Appia antica' and discover the time of the great emperors on a relaxed tour far away from mass tourism and

crowded streets. Sundays are best for this, as the Via Appia is then closed to cars! You can find more information about this at: www.romaculta.com

Suggestion 2: Go to the 'Largo di Torre Argentina'. In the middle of this square is the 'Area Sacra', an excavation site of the sacred district. There you can see the remains of several ancient temples. The whole area is located slightly below the current street level and is home to the Cat Forum for stray cats, so there is plenty on offer here for animal lovers and visitors interested in history. You will also learn how important cats have always been to the Romans. Further information is available at: www.romancats.com

CHRISTIAN ROME

Now you already know a great deal about the rise and fall of ancient Rome, as well as the times of the kingdom, republic and empire. But how did the city rise again and become what we know it as today?

After the fall of Rome as a glorious empire, it only regained its importance from 800 AD, when it initially became the capital of the Papal States (Latin 'Patrimonium Petri') and thus the most important place of pilgrimage for Christians alongside Santiago de Compostela and Jerusalem.

In addition, Charlemagne (Latin 'Carolus Magnus') was crowned Holy Roman Emperor by Pope Leo III. In the period between the 8th and 11th centuries, Rome suffered many lootings, sieges and attacks. Around 800, there were only just under 20,000 inhabitants left in the city. Entire districts became deserted and the cityscape was now characterized by densely populated ('abitato') and uninhabited ('disabitato') districts. Small settlements mostly formed near Rome's large churches.

This brings us to Christian Rome. And Christian Rome also has its origins in a legend. According to tradition, the apostle Peter preached in what was then Rome, the center of the world. When he wanted to leave the city for fear of the persecution of Christians, he met Jesus on the Via Appia and Peter asked him: "Lord, where are you going?" (Latin: "Domine, quo vadis?"). And Jesus answered him: 'I am going to be crucified a second time'. (Latin 'Venio iterum crucifigi'). Thus the church

Domine quo vadis was built on the site of their meeting on the Via Appia.

Peter also returned to Rome, where he became the first bishop of the Christian community until he died a martyr's death in 63 AD. Soon after, a veritable cult developed around his tomb and when Constantine the Great finally recognized Christianity in the Edict of Milan in 313, he commissioned the construction of the first St. Peter's Church directly above this tomb, the high altar of which is still located right above Peter's tomb today.

When visiting Rome, you should definitely not miss St. Peter's Basilica, because here you can marvel at one of the largest and most beautiful churches in the world. At the same time, you will also find many works of art by famous artists such as Michelangelo, Raphael and Bernini in St. Peter's Basilica.

Another very important church in Rome is the Lateran Basilica ('San Giovanni in Laterano'), as it is regarded as the mother and head (Latin 'mater et caput') of all churches in Rome and throughout the world.

There are a total of seven of these papal basilicas in Rome. These include San Giovanni in Laterano (= Lateran Basilica), San Pietro in Vaticano (= St. Peter's Basilica) and San Paolo fuori le mura (= St. Paul Outside the Walls),

Santa Maria Maggiore (= the largest Marian church in the city), San Lorenzo fuori le mura (= St. Lawrence outside the walls), Santa Croce Gerusalemme (= pilgrims' church) and San Sebastiano fuori le mura (= pilgrims' church).

In fact, there are countless churches in Rome, so it is impossible to list them all. However, one of the oldest churches in Rome should not go unmentioned: the Basilica of Santa Maria di Trastevere, which dates back to the early Christian period of the 12th century. If you have any free time during your stay in Rome, be sure to use it for a detour to this church!

Peter is therefore considered the first bishop of Rome. However, the first designation as pope (Latin 'papa'), which originally meant 'father', goes back to Bishop Siricius of Rome (385-399 AD). It was Pope Gregory I (in office from 590-604) who finally wrote this official title for the Bishop of Rome into law.

The cityscape of Rome, characterized by the many churches that were built back then, has been preserved to this day and many pilgrims travel to Rome every year to experience this atmosphere. Especially at Easter and Christmas, when the Pope gives the blessing 'Urbi et Orbi', countless visitors come to Rome.

Explore Christian Rome

Christian Rome can also be explored in many different ways. Here are two small ideas that you are welcome to try out.

Task 1: Find the place in St. Peter's Basilica where Emperor Charles was crowned!

Task 2: Attend a church service in Rome! German church services are held, for example, in the Church of St. Maria della Pietà on the Campo Santo Teutonico. The services are usually at 7.00 a.m. and 9.00 a.m., groups should register in advance: www.camposanto.va

Rome today is very diverse. You will be amazed at how effortlessly ancient buildings, Christian places of worship and modern buildings blend together to form a harmonious cityscape. But the most important thing is that Rome represents one thing above all: The city is living and breathing history!

Let us therefore conclude the historical part of this book with how Rome finally became the city you will find when you visit.

Now that Rome had become a Papal State, you are probably wondering how it could then become the capital of Italy. The answer will amaze you, because you could almost say that parts of history that had already happened were repeating themselves!

In 1849, Rome was occupied by French troops, but these were withdrawn in 1870 when France declared war on Prussia. As a result, the Italian military seized the opportunity to march into Rome with almost no resistance and deprive the Pope of his power.

Thus, on January 26, 1871, Rome was named the capital of the Italian nation state, which emerged as a kingdom. This period between 1815 and 1870 is also known in Italian as the 'Risorgimento' (= 'resurrection'). This era is particularly visible in the city through the national monument 'Monumento Nazionale a Vittorio Emmanuele II', inaugurated in 1911 and built for the king of the same name.

It is also worth noting that Rome's population began to grow rapidly again at this time, as many inhabitants of rural regions moved back into the city, so that for the first time since antiquity Rome's city limits once again extended beyond the Aurelian Wall.

However, many Catholics were hostile to this new development for a long time and it was only after the First World War that Benito Mussolini, who had brought Italy under fascist rule since 1922, succeeded in reconciling state and church in 1929 with the Lateran Treaties. As a result, the independent state of Vatican City (Vatican City for short) was created.

At the same time, many ancient buildings are being restored, as antiquity is being glorified for propaganda purposes.

In the ensuing period of the Second World War, Rome was also initially bombed, but Pope Pius XII remained in the city and endeavored to have Rome declared an 'open city'. This meant that Rome would not defend itself and the city could therefore not be (further) bombed or attacked. In 1944, this proposal was accepted by German troops and allied troops marched into Rome. Finally, in 1946, King Umberto II was the last Italian king to leave Rome and Italy once again became a republic.

Like German cities, Rome subsequently experienced a strong economic upturn in the post-war years and an enormous increase in population. From the 1960s onwards, entire large housing estates were built and a little earlier, in 1955, the 'Metropolitana di Roma', Rome's first subway line, was opened.

The 1970s in Rome, on the other hand, were unfortunately often characterized by social struggles, squats, strikes and political violence. The high point of this was the kidnapping and murder of Italian Prime Minister Aldo Moro by the underground organization the 'Red Brigades'. It was not until the 1980s that the situation in Rome eased again, as some of the inhabitants moved out of the city.

To find newer buildings in Rome, you have to go to the outskirts of the city, as many areas in the center are rightly listed. This also often makes it difficult to build new buildings in the city center - if you want to - as excavations often reveal further archaeological finds. Unfortunately, the outer districts and suburbs still have a high crime rate and are also poorly connected to public transport and therefore to the city center.

In the city center, on the other hand, many of the apartments are privately owned and very well maintained. There are therefore hardly any rental apartments in the center of Rome.

Incidentally, the highlights of Rome in modern times can all be dated back to the pontificate of Pope John Paul II. Rome welcomed around 2 million visitors to World Youth Day in 2000 and the funeral of Pope John Paul II in 2005 was attended by as many as 3-4 million guests and 200 heads of state and government.

<u>Explore the Rome of today</u>

Now go on a little discovery tour through modern-day Rome. As the Vatican is an independent state in its own right, it also has its own post office and letterboxes.

Probably the most controversial building in Rome, however, is the 'Monumento Nazionale a Vittorio Emmanuele II'. In the Roman vernacular, it is often referred to as the 'typewriter of Rome', as the external shape of this building is sometimes reminiscent of a very oversized typewriter.

<u>Task 1</u>: Write and send a postcard from the Vatican! At the same time, write and send a postcard using the Roman postal system and then see which card arrives faster!

<u>Task 2</u>: Visit the national monument 'Monumento Nazionale a Vittorio Emmanuele II', which is located in Piazza Venezia.

Arrival and accommodation

Now that we've finished the historical part of this book and you've read a lot about Rome and have certainly grown fond of the city, you're probably wondering how you can get to Rome.

A proverb literally says 'Many roads lead to Rome' and what in our everyday life only means that there are many different ways to reach your destination, this also applies in practice to your travel preparations, because if you want to visit the Eternal City, there are various ways to get there.

ARRIVAL BY TRAIN

If you want to travel to Rome by train, a lot depends on your starting point. It also depends on how experienced you are in buying and booking tickets.

If this is not a problem for you, you can simply order your train ticket online by entering your departure point and your desired destination as well as the departure date and time. You should then be able to book a return journey yourself in the same way.

If, on the other hand, you are not so confident in using online booking systems, it is best to seek advice at your local DB travel center and buy your tickets there.

Plan enough time for your journey in any case, as there are usually no direct connections, so you may have to change trains (several times). It is always worth looking out for rail savings offers and seeing if you can take a night train (e.g. from Munich) - this often saves time, money and nerves!

Rome's main train station is called 'Roma Termini' and is centrally located in the city. If you want, you can rent a car there directly. There are also numerous useful facilities in the central station, such as a tourist information office, ticket services, a post office and even a medical care center.

www.romatermini.com
Pro:
- Relaxed arrival
- Also suitable for people with a fear of flying
Contra:
- Too time-consuming for a short stay in Rome

ARRIVAL BY CAR

If you intend to travel to Rome by car, you are very flexible in the overall organization of your trip at any time.

You can set off whenever you want and take as much luggage with you as will fit in the car. The journey is also easy to manage with children, as you can take as many breaks as you want or need.

The only factor to consider when traveling to Italy by car is time, so it can sometimes make sense to plan an overnight stopover halfway through the journey.

It is also important to know that most Italian highways are subject to tolls. You will receive the necessary tickets when you enter a toll station. You can also find out about the tickets, tariffs and payment systems in advance from the ADAC.

Overall, traveling to Rome by car is relatively relaxed, but it can become a little more stressful as soon as you reach the actual city area of Rome. Here you often have to expect a lot of traffic, although the Romans themselves are quite patient drivers.

Just like at home, it is best to avoid the morning and afternoon rush hours. There is a three-lane ring highway around Rome, the 'Grande Raccordo Anulare' (abbreviated GRA or A 90), this highway is toll-free just like the highway to the airport and runs completely around Rome.

You should also bear in mind that there are also many small streets and alleyways in Rome itself, where the traffic is even heavier. However, if you are not put off by the possible shortage of parking spaces, you can look forward to a very individual trip through the Eternal City!

Pro:

- Individual and flexible travel

- Mobility at all times

Contra:

- Toll costs

- z. Lots of traffic in the urban area

ARRIVAL BY PLANE

The easiest and quickest way to travel to Rome is by plane.

Rome has a total of three airports. The largest and most modern airport is Rome-Fiumicino Airport, named after the small town of Fiumicino, which is very close by. However, the official name of this airport is 'Aeroporto di Roma-Fiumicino Leonardo da Vinci'. It is located around 33 km from the city center and is not only the largest airport in Rome, but also in the whole of Italy. It is therefore sometimes hectic and crowded, which can spoil the first impression of a relaxing vacation. One plus point, however, is that there is a direct train connection to the city center. From Fiumicino Airport, the FL 1 line will take you to the city center or the main train station.

The second largest airport in Rome is 'Rome-Ciampino', officially called 'Aeroporto di Roma-Ciampino Giovan Battista Pastine'. It is located approx. 15 km outside the city center. If you are arriving in Rome on a so-called 'budget flight', then it is very likely that you will land here. This airport also has a train connection to the city center. It is best to take the FL 4 line to Roma Termini.

Last but not least, there is a third, very small airport in Rome called 'Rome-Urbe'. Although it is only 8 km from the city center, it is hardly relevant for tourists, as mainly small planes and helicopters take off and land here for sightseeing flights over Rome.

From Fiumicino and Ciampino airports, you can also reach the city center by shuttle bus and cab.

www.adr.it/fiumicino
www.adr.it/ciampino

Pro:

- Great time savings

Contra:

- Not suitable for travelers with a fear of flying
- Sometimes a bit hectic at large airports

ARRIVAL BY BOAT

If you want to make your visit to Rome even more adventurous, you can also reach the city by boat - often as part of a cruise.

The cruise ships usually dock in the port of Civitavecchia. From here, Rome is about 80 km away!

In Civitavecchia, you then have various options for getting to Rome: For example, there is the option of booking an excursion to Rome with one of the many providers directly at the dock, if this is not already included in the cruise itinerary.

However, it is much cheaper to discover the city on your own and travel to Rome by train. Regional trains run from Civitavecchia station to Rome approximately every half hour and take around 45 minutes to Roma Termini central station.

However, with this option it could be even more interesting to travel only as far as Roma San Pietro (approx. 30 minutes) and from there go to the Vatican and visit it.

You can find more exciting information for day trips to Rome at: www.meine-landaus-fluege.de

Pro:

- A day trip organized as part of a package is particularly suitable for a first visit to get to know Rome.

Contra:

- With cruises, you usually have little room for maneuver in the itinerary.

THE 3 BEST HOTELS IN ROME

In this section you will find three suggestions on how to stay during your stay in Rome.

It should be noted that Rome is very hospitable and has at least as many hotels as churches.

In addition, the choice of accommodation is always very subjective, as every traveler has their own ideas and needs regarding their accommodation, so it is almost impossible to please everyone.

My selection within Rome was therefore based on the criteria of accessibility, simplicity and proximity to the city center.

However, if these hotel suggestions are not to your liking, you can easily find many other alternatives in the city.

Allora, let's start with the first proposal.

<u>Casa per Ferie Santa Maria alle Fornaci:</u>
This special guest house is very centrally located in Rome not far from St. Peter's Basilica and was originally a monastery with an adjoining church.

It has been extensively renovated in recent years and now offers small but nice single and double rooms, each with its own bathroom. W-LAN and an extensive breakfast buffet round off the basic service of this hotel very well. The reception is manned 24 hours a day and you feel safe and in good hands at all times. Due to its proximity to the center, it is ideally located for exploring Rome on foot.

Other services include an airport shuttle, luggage storage and accessibility.

www.santamariafornaci.com

The Beehive Hostel Rome:

This guest house was founded in 1999 and is also very centrally located, very close to Rome's main train station.

It has a range of accommodation options from shared rooms with shared bathroom facilities to single and double rooms with private bathrooms.

The overall atmosphere here is very informal and sociable. Vegetarian meals are also available for guests.

There are also regular communal cooking evenings and city tours, so you'll never be alone for long, but can still find plenty of peace and quiet.

www.the-beehive.com

<u>**Hostel Trustever:**</u>

This hostel is located in the trendy Trastevere district and has various accommodation options consisting of double, triple and multi-bed rooms. All rooms have a private bathroom and Wi-Fi.

The hostel mainly appeals to younger (back-packing) tourists. It has its own launderette and lockable luggage lockers and is open 24 hours a day.

Meals can be booked individually.

www.hosteltrustever.com

Important sights in Rome

In this chapter, I would like to take a closer look at some of Rome's most important sights with you. In a city as big as Rome, you will never manage to see everything in just one visit, but there is always something new to discover on your next visit.

This preselection should serve as an introductory guide, especially for your first visit to the Eternal City.

Roman Forum

The Roman Forum was built between the 5th and 7th centuries AD and was continuously expanded. It experienced its heyday during the imperial era and was considered the cultural, economic, religious and political power center of ancient Rome.

Today, the Roman Forum is one of the most important excavation sites in the city and allows you to marvel at the remains of the triumphal arch of Emperor Septimius Severus, the Temple of Saturn, the Curia, the Basilica of Emperor Constantine and the Temple of Vesta.

From the Capitoline Hill you can get a particularly good and comprehensive overview of the Roman Forum.

Palatine

The Palatine Hill is one of the famous seven hills of Rome. It is the oldest inhabited part of the city and is associated with a long history. The Palatine is even considered to be the place where Romulus originally founded Rome. Later, the Roman upper class lived here and many emperors resided here.

Today you can still find the remains of ancient temples dedicated to Magna Marta, Victoria and Apollo on the Palatine Hill. The palace complex of Domitian can also still be seen.

To get an even better idea of life in those days, you can also visit the Palatine Museum.

Colosseum

The Colosseum is the largest amphitheater in ancient Rome, it could seat up to 50,000 people and was the scene of countless gruesome gladiator fights. It was built from around 72 to 79 AD on the orders of Emperor Vespasian. The opening ceremony is said to have lasted 100 days.

The free citizens of Rome had free entry to the Colosseum and the games were part of the political campaign 'bread and circuses' (lat. 'panem et circenses'), which served to keep the Romans calm and content.

When Christianity became the official religion of the Roman Empire in 313 AD, Emperor Constantine banned the fights, but they continued to take place until the last gladiator fights were finally held in 523 AD. After that, the Colosseum was used as a fortress and even as a quarry!

Today it is the symbol of Rome and is recognized as a masterpiece of ancient architecture.

Via Appia

The Via Appia was the most famous and most important long-distance and trade route in ancient Rome and led over 540 kilometers to Brindisi. Its construction began in 312 AD under Appius Claudius Caesus.

The street was lined with villas, tombs and catacombs, the ruins of which still remain today.

The historical part of this road is therefore known as 'Via Appia Antica'. The remaining section is partly hidden under a modern road surface and is known as 'Via Appia Nuova' or 'State Road 7 (SS7)'.

It is best to visit the Via Appia on Sundays, when it is closed to cars and is ideal for relaxed discovery tours.

Ostia Antica

Ostia Antica is the name given to the original port city of ancient Rome, located around 23 kilometers from today's city center at the mouth of the Tiber.

Ostia Antica was founded in the 4th century BC as a Roman colony and was initially mainly a military camp for the protection of Rome, which then quickly developed into a port city. The most important commodity at the time was grain, which was brought to Rome from Africa to feed the Roman citizens.

At the same time as the ancient city of Rome fell, Ostia Antica also lost its importance, as the port city was no longer needed due to Rome's steadily decreasing population.

Today, however, Ostia Antica is also one of the most important excavation sites of ancient Rome. There is a museum there and you can also marvel at the remains of theaters, thermal baths, the forum, latrines and stores as well as many tombs.

Imperial Forums

The Imperial Forums are an extension of the Roman Forum, which had quickly become too small during the heyday of Ancient Rome and no longer met the requirements of many emperors.

A total of four additional imperial forums were therefore added to the Forum Romanum. These are the Forum Iulium, which is also known as the Caesar Forum, the Forum of Augustus, the Transitorium, which also bears the name Nerva Forum, and the Forum of Trajan.

The Forum Iulium was the first of the four extensions and was commissioned by Gaius Iulius Caesar from 54 BC. With its rectangular shape, it resembled the public squares in Greece and had the Temple of Venus Genetrix on one narrow side.

The Forum of Augustus was built around 50 years later and was similar in structure to the Forum of Caesar. However, the temple of Mars Ultor formed the center here, which also stood for the importance of this forum: everything that had to do with war and victory was decided here!

In 71-75 AD, Emperor Vespasian had a temple of peace built on the site, the 'Templum Pacis', to celebrate the end of the civil wars and peace. This was very similar to the other forums, so much so that it was sometimes referred to as an additional 'Forum Pacis'.

Finally, Emperor Domitian had another forum, the Nerva Forum, built on the open space between the temple and the Forum of Augustus. As it was not completed during his lifetime, it was named after his successor Emperor Nerva in 97 AD and because it combined the previous buildings into a single unit, it was soon referred to as the 'Transitorium'.

The Forum of Trajan was then built as the last imperial forum from 107 to 112 AD. It is considered the most magnificent and largest forum and was also adorned in the middle by Trajan's Column. The Basilica Ulpia was also located at the rear of the square.

Many of the forums are only partially visible today, as Mussolini had this area built over with the Via dei Fiori Imperiali without first having it archaeologically examined.

Circus Maximus

The Circus Maximus was the largest arena in the heyday of ancient Rome and the venue for chariot races (lat. 'ludi circenses') until the 6th century AD.

At times, the stands could accommodate between 150,000 and 250,000 people and the total length was 600 meters.

Initially, it was still a wooden construction and it was only in 46 BC that Gaius Iulius Caesar had marble benches installed for his triumphal games.

As a rule, 7 laps had to be driven during a race and in the heyday of the empire, 12 to 24 races were held per day. These were public events that were usually held as part of celebrations and were financed by the state.

Just like the Colosseum, the Circus Maximus also hosted gladiator fights and animal hunts, and athletic competitions based on the Greek model were also an integral part of the program.

After the fall of Ancient Rome, the Circus Maximus also fell into disrepair and the area was used for various purposes. Parts of the benches were even used for the construction of St. Peter's Basilica.

Excavations were then carried out on the site from 1936 and today it is mainly used for large events such as concerts. Since 2016, there has been a small exhibition there with information about the Circus Maximus.

Caracalla Thermal Baths

The Baths of Caracalla also date back to antiquity and are among the largest thermal baths in Rome. The construction was commissioned by Emperor Septimius Severus in 206 and the baths were completed in 216 during the reign of Emperor Caracalla.

These were public and admission-free bathing facilities that were intended to increase the emperor's popularity among the common people.

The baths are said to have been in operation until the 5th century, when Theodoric the Great ruled Rome. After that, they were partly destroyed during sieges of Rome or were exposed to the forces of nature. Later, they were also used as quarries or to decorate other buildings.

Today, the thermal baths can be toured by visitors using VR glasses so that you can see exactly what everything looked like back then. Otherwise, the thermal baths are mainly used for opera performances.

IN CHRISTIAN ROME

St. Peter's Basilica
St. Peter's Basilica (it. 'San Pietro in Vaticano') is one of the largest and certainly one of the most important churches in the world for Christianity. It is one of the seven pilgrimage churches in Rome and is the largest papal basilica. A total of 20,000 people can be accommodated in St. Peter's Basilica.

The church was originally commissioned by Constantine the Great in around 324 AD so that a place of worship could be built over the presumed burial site of the Apostle Peter. St. Peter's Basilica in its current form was built from 1506 and completed in 1626.

It forms the heart of the Vatican and is a must-see during your visit to Rome!

Castel Sant'Angelo

Castel Santangelo is a place at least as steeped in history as St. Peter's Basilica. It was originally built as a mausoleum for the Roman Emperor Hadrian and his successors, but was soon converted into a fortress by the popes and used in this function until 1901 as a place of refuge for the popes in the event of imminent danger in Rome. At times, Castel Sant'Angelo also served as a prison for the popes.

Castel Sant'Angelo was given its name in 590, because at that time the plague was raging in Rome and Pope Gregory I (Gregory the Great) is said to have seen the archangel Michael above the castle, who prophesied the end of the plague, which came to pass shortly afterwards. For this reason, there is still an angel at the top of the castle today.

Since 1906, Castel Sant'Angelo has been a museum, which you can visit and which gives you an insight into this part of Rome's history. From the platform of Castel Sant'Angelo you also have a spectacular view of the Eternal City.

Pantheon

The Pantheon is another Roman building from antiquity. Construction of the Pantheon began under Emperor Trajan in 114 AD and was completed during the reign of Emperor Hadrian between 125 and 128 AD. At that time, it was a sanctuary in which statues of various deities were erected and which was dedicated to all the gods.

In 609 AD, the Pantheon was finally converted into a Christian church and is now a Roman Catholic church with the official name 'Santa Maria ad Martyres'. Due to an earlier common name variant as 'Sancta Maria Rotonda' and the round shape of the building, the building in Rome is now popularly known as 'La Rotonda'.

For a long time, the Pantheon as a building also had the largest dome in the world and is still one of the best preserved buildings of antiquity. There is a round opening in the dome of the Pantheon, which has a diameter of 9 meters, and yet you will find that it is never wet inside, even when it rains, because the floor slopes towards the middle and is equipped with drains.

This masterpiece of architectural architecture alone should prompt you to plan a visit to the Pantheon into your stay in Rome.

The Pantheon is also the burial place of many famous artists, such as the painter Raphael.

Vatican Museums

In the Vatican Museums, art lovers can discover true treasures from antiquity to the Middle Ages to the Renaissance and much more. It is a collection of several museums, all of which are located in different parts of the Vatican Palace. The founder of this collection is said to have been Pope Julius II, who began acquiring various sculptures from around 1506.

In the years that followed, the papal palace was continuously expanded so that today it comprises around 1400 rooms on an area of 55,000 square meters, the majority of this complex is open to the public and only a small part is reserved for the Pope and his entourage. The most famous part of these museums is the Sistine Chapel.

Sistine Chapel

The Sistine Chapel (it. 'Capella Sistina') is part of the papal palace. It was built between 1475 and 1483 by order of its namesake Pope Sixtus IV and houses many famous paintings, including works by Botticelli and Michelangelo.

The ceiling paintings by Michelangelo are particularly famous, as they depict scenes from Genesis and the section entitled 'The Creation of Adam' is certainly the most copied work of this period and is world-famous.

The Sistine Chapel is where the conclave takes place whenever a new pope has to be elected. However, visitors can only enter the Sistine Chapel through the Vatican Museums.
Vatican employees, on the other hand, can have their children baptized in the Sistine Chapel, which is certainly a special feature.

Trevi Fountain

The Trevi Fountain (it. 'Fontana di Trevi') is the crowd puller of the Eternal City and one of the most important sights when you visit Rome.

Originally, an aqueduct ended at this point in ancient Rome, which ensured the water supply for the thermal baths in this part of the city through three springs. In addition, three streets (it. 'tre vie') meet at this square, so that these two approaches could be responsible for the naming of the fountain.

In its current form, the Trevi Fountain was commissioned by Pope Clement XII and designed by the architect Nicola Salvi around 1732 and finally completed by Giuseppe Pannini in 1762. The central focus of the fountain is a depiction of the god Oceanus. The Trevi Fountain is the largest fountain in Rome!

For many years, the legend has also persisted that you have to throw a coin over your shoulder into the fountain if you want to return safely to Rome. In this way, huge sums of money are collected every year, which the city of Rome donates to charities such as Caritas.

Spanish Steps

The Spanish Steps (it. 'Scalinata di Trinità dei Monti') is the connection between the Piazza di Spagna and the French church 'Santa Trinità dei Monti'. It was given the German name 'Spanische Treppe' because it is located in the Piazza di Spagna, where the Spanish embassy is also located.

It was built from 1723 at the request of Pope Innocent XIII and the French King Louis XII, who wanted a dignified ascent to the church he was financing. The competition between royal and papal interests is also reflected in the design of the staircase, which can be seen in the symbols of lilies (for the king) and eagles (for the pope). The leading architect in the construction was Francesco De Sanctis. The staircase has a total of 138 steps.

Today, the Spanish Steps are a very popular photo motif for tourists and a much-visited meeting place, and the fashion industry also often uses this backdrop to hold fashion shows on the

Spanish Steps. This is mainly due to the fact that the steps are not far from Via Condotti, Rome's fashion mile.

Piazza Navona

If you are looking for a lively square in Rome at any time of day, then you will find it in Piazza Navona. Piazza Navona symbolizes a typical baroque square in the Eternal City and is adorned with three fountains.

Originally, there was a stadium for sporting competitions on this site in ancient times, based on the Greek model, which explains the elongated oval shape of the square.

During the Baroque period, the square was completely redesigned in the style of the ancient imperial forums. This resulted in the three fountains that still exist on the square today: the Fountain of the Moors (it. 'Fontana del Moro') to the south, the Fountain of Neptune (it. 'Fontana del Nettuno') to the north and the Fountain of the Four Rivers (it. 'Fontana dei Quattro Fiumi') in the middle.

All three fountains were created or redesigned by the famous sculptor and architect Bernini. The centerpiece of the square is the Fountain of the Four Rivers, which was created around 1650 and whose impressive four sculptures represent the most important rivers in the world at the time. The Danube stands for Europe, the Ganges symbolizes Asia, the Nile embodies Africa and the Rio della Plata is the symbol of America.

Another highlight of Piazza Navona is the Church of Sant'Agnese, also built by Borromini around 1650.

Today, Piazza Navona is surrounded by numerous cafés and street artists and lots of hawkers dominate the scene, making the square a real tourist attraction.

Trastevere
The Trastevere district (Latin 'trans Tiberim' = 'beyond the Tiber'), which is located on the other side of the Tiber, exudes a very special flair for tourists and locals alike.

It was once the district of workers, immigrants and other marginalized groups before it was increasingly developed for tourism. Trastevere is home to one of the oldest Christian churches in Rome, the church of Santa Maria in Trastevere.

Today you get the feeling that Trastevere is still a village in the city, and the image of the district is characterized by a lot of culture and gastronomy, which invites you to linger and enjoy.

INSIDER TIPS

In this chapter, you will now find two further suggestions that should enable you to delve even deeper into the history of Rome. But before we get to that point, I would also like to give you two general tips that can be useful for all the visits and activities you will be doing in the Eternal City.

Tip 1: Public toilets With so many sightseeing tours, it is inevitable that you will need a public toilet at some point. Without local knowledge, it can sometimes be difficult to find one straight away. Therefore, use the website https://pee.place.de to display the public toilets - it also works for Rome!

<u>Tip 2</u>: Pickpockets You often read that there are many pickpockets in Rome. However, this does not mean that every tourist in the city is mugged or robbed. Nevertheless, always keep an eye on your luggage and bags!

When sightseeing, it is advisable to have a bag or rucksack that closes well. You can also carry these well and clearly in front of your body in large crowds!
Chest pouches have also always proved their worth for valuables!

Let us now return to the proposals already mentioned.

Domus Aurea

After the fire in Rome in 64 AD, Emperor Nero had a kind of transitional house built on the site of the former palace - the 'Domus Transitoria' - a new palace called the 'Domus Aurea' (Latin for the Golden House). This building was more of an estate than a palace, it had more than 300 rooms and the total area was around 80 hectares. It got its name from the fact that all the ceilings and walls were painted on the inside and covered with marble, ivory, semi-precious stones and even gold. This made it the most extravagant building in the history of Rome.

Today, after many years of extensive restoration work, the Domus Aurea is once again open to tourists and can only be visited by booking a guided tour. The special thing about this is that the guided tours are conducted using virtual reality, so that you have the opportunity to explore Nero's palace in all its splendor and fully immerse yourself in this exciting time!

Crypt of the Capuchins
You can experience another exciting, but also somewhat bizarre sightseeing tour in another church in Rome. The Capuchins are a branch of the Franciscan monks and got their name from the fact that they always wore a habit with a hood covering their heads.

The church 'Santa Maria Immacolata a Via Veneto' or 'Nostra Signora della Concezione dei Cappuccini' (= Our Lady of the Conception of the Capuchins) was built between 1626 and 1631 by order of Cardinal Antonio Barberini, the brother of Pope Urban VIII.

In the crypt of this church, Cardinal Barberini then had an ossuary created from the remains of thousands of deceased monks by artfully rearranging them into wall decorations and biblical depictions. In total, the remains of around 3600 friars who were buried between 1500 and 1870 rest here in this way.

Today you can visit the museum there, which also houses a depiction of St. Francis by Caravaggio and a painting by Guido Reni depicting the Archangel Michael, and then explore the crypt, which consists of several rooms.

If you are not put off by the (Latin) message 'Quod fuimus, estis, quod sumus, eritis', which could be translated as 'We were what you are, and what we are, you will be', you can visit the museum daily from 9 am to 7 pm. www.capucciniviaveneto.it

Food and drink

After so much information and impressions, aren't you starting to get hungry? Then let's go out for something to eat!

WORTH KNOWING

Italian restaurants are very different from those in Germany. The first thing you will notice when you arrive in Rome is that there is usually a waiter outside the door. His job is to approach people on the street and win them over as guests - sometimes in a very persistent manner!

In addition, you will very often be shown to a free seat in the restaurant by a waiter, so you will rarely be able to choose a seat yourself. In most cases, eating in restaurants is also associated with a certain price for the place setting.

You will notice this particularly clearly if you want to go for a coffee. If you drink it in a restaurant, it will be more expensive than if you drink it directly at the bar.

> <u>Tip 1:</u> Always drink your coffee at the bar! (it. 'al banco')

Many of the restaurants in Rome have a menu in Italian and English. If there is only an Italian menu, just let yourself be surprised - you are guaranteed to find something delicious!

> <u>Tip 2:</u> Be sure to try a classic Roman specialty: Roman-style artichokes (it. 'Carciofi alla Romana')
>
> Attention! There are many street vendors in Rome who pretend to want to give you something (e.g. a handmade bracelet). Please don't

give in to this, as the vendors usually expect you to buy them a coffee or something similar!

And do you know the difference between Neapolitan and Roman pizza? Neapolitan pizza has a very thin base and the classic round shape. If you order a Roman pizza, on the other hand, you often get a rectangular pizza with a much thicker base. Try it out for yourself!

THE 3 BEST RESTAURANTS IN ROME

I would now like to suggest three restaurants where you will find much of what makes Rome special. Of course, there are numerous other places here too, so the city has something to offer for every taste.

1. <u>alterNATIVO drink&food:</u> This small bistro is located in Piazza di Santa Maria alle Fornaci 21-22 and invites you to enjoy cozy evenings with good wine and lots of delicious snacks. It is ideal for anyone who likes to dine in a somewhat alternative ambience and a tranquil but modern atmosphere.

2. <u>Hostaria I Quattro Mori:</u> This restaurant is located at Via di Santa Maria alle Fornaci 8 and is considered the favorite restaurant of some clergymen and even the Pope! Here you will find many delicious Mediterranean dishes and a wide range of fish and meat dishes, which you can enjoy in a friendly and relaxed atmosphere.

3. <u>La Fraschetta: If you want to enjoy</u> a really classic Italian meal and also want the typical ambience of an Italian restaurant, then La Fraschetta in Via di San Francesco a Ripa 134 in the Trastevere district is the place for you. Here you can get everything from pasta to pizza, which is a must when visiting Rome!

ALTERNATIVES

However, if you don't have that much time to eat or just want a snack between meals so that you can see more of the city, there is also the perfect alternative. There are many food trucks in Rome that offer delicious hot or cold sandwiches that are quick and reasonably priced.

This option is also very suitable if you get hungry during a city tour or if you are traveling in a group and only have short breaks between your program points.

Shopping in Rome

Fashion, shopping, lots of souvenirs and many other souvenirs from the Vatican - Rome is also known for this and you will never be embarrassed not to know what to bring back from this vacation, because the selection is once again huge! So be sure to plan enough time to browse through the many stores and numerous stores!

FASHION

Fashion enthusiasts will find a little paradise in Rome. To show you the best places to store, I would like to present 3 different areas of the

Eternal City below, so that you have a better over-view and can proceed according to your shopping preferences.

As you will remember, I already mentioned Via Condotti in the introduction to this book. This is the place to be if you are looking for the big brands and designers of Italian fashion, as this street is lined with one boutique after the next and you can buy designer fashion from Giorgio Armani, Versace, Gucci, Dolce e Gabbana, Bulgari or Valentino. But even if you don't want to buy anything here, it's still worth simply strolling through the street and admiring the window displays. It is not for nothing that the Romans themselves call this street 'Chic & Shock Street', as every woman is guaranteed to be able to dress elegantly and chicly here, but the man will suffer a little shock when paying afterwards! ☺

Via Condotti is therefore located in the district known as 'Tridente' and consists of three converging (main) streets, namely Via di Ripetta, Via del Corso and Via del Babuino. You can store to your heart's content in all of these streets and Piazza di Spagna with the Spanish Steps is also located here. Many ateliers and jewelry stores have set up shop in this square and many of the stores there are dedicated exclusively to Alta Moda.

If, on the other hand, you prefer modern, well-known shopping chains such as H&M, Zara or Benetton, you will find them on the lower part of Via del Corso, in the direction of Piazza Venezia. There is also the large shopping gallery 'Galleria Alberto Sordi', where you can discover brands such as Bershka or Calvin Klein. A visit to the gallery is also worthwhile, as it has not been changed since 1922.

However, if you are not interested in modern or new clothes, but are looking for second-hand stores, you might be particularly interested in the 'Monti' district. Here you will mainly find small vintage and design stores and antique stores in the many alleyways. The streets Via del Governo vecchio and Via del Boschetto are particularly worth seeing. There are also lots of flea markets here at weekends.

Extra tip: In Rome - as is often the case throughout Italy - you can buy beautifully crafted and very elegant genuine leather shoes at very reasonable prices, an opportunity not to be missed!

Most stores in Rome open at around 10 am and close between 8 and 9 pm. Smaller stores may take a lunch break (it. 'siesta').

SOUVENIRS AND POST

If you want to buy souvenirs in Rome, you don't have to look far. There are numerous souvenir stores in the city center and plenty of opportunities to buy the right vacation souvenir.

However, if you would like to send postcards from Rome, you have several options. Firstly, you can send postcards from the Vatican in Rome. Vatican post is considered to be particularly fast and reliable. However, it is important to note that the Vatican's postal service is a separate system and has its own letterboxes and post offices directly in St. Peter's Square.

Alternatively, you can also send your mail via the normal Italian postal system. In this case, however, you should choose the 'Posta Prioritaria' to speed up delivery. Incidentally, the letterboxes in Rome are generally red for domestic mail and blue for international mail. You can either buy stamps directly at the post office or in one of the many tobacco stores (it. 'Tabacchi').

<u>Attention</u>! For some years now, so-called GPS stamps have been available in Rome. If you frank your postcards with them, you are supposed to be able to track the postal route of your cards. These cards can then only be posted in special yellow post boxes.
The fact is that the Italian postal service does not actually accept GPS mail and that this is more of a dubious and overpriced business model!

DEVOTIONAL OBJECTS

If you intend to take religious souvenirs with you from Rome, it is best to buy them directly from the Vatican. There are smaller stores there that are attached to St. Peter's Basilica, for example.

If, on the other hand, you would like a somewhat larger selection, we recommend the 'Mondo Cattolico' store right on the border with the Vatican. Here you will find a well-stocked range of rosaries, mosaics, statues, crosses, medals and other great devotional items and you can also buy the coveted holy water there.

www.mondocattolico.it

FOOD

In Rome, it is very easy to stock up on food for your daily needs. There are many kiosks that sell drinks and a small range of food. In addition, there is also the supermarket chain 'Carrefour' in the city. In these stores you will also find many items that you are familiar with from home.

You also have the unique opportunity to buy fresh fruit and vegetables at the weekly markets. A particularly beautiful market takes place every morning (except Sundays) on the Campo de Fiori.

<u>ATTENTION</u>: Please do not buy drinking water bottles from the countless hawkers in Rome. These bottles are often already refilled with contaminated water, which is why the Romans commonly refer to this water as 'mouse water'!

However, there are many drinking fountains in Rome where you can safely refill your bottles and which are specially designed for this purpose.

Conversation

Even if you are traveling to Rome for the first time and don't speak Italian, you don't have to worry about communication.

You can derive many things in Rome from other languages (Italian, for example, is still very similar to Latin). In addition, many young people in Rome also speak English. The city is also always prepared for its many visitors, so that at least at many of the sights the signage is also multilingual. Apart from that, there are always ways and means of communicating.

Nevertheless, it's always nice to know at least a few sentences and important phrases in the local language - sometimes this proves to be a lifesaver!

In general, Italians also like it when you make an effort to speak Italian.

GREETING

Hello / Bye! = Ciao!
Good morning! = Buon giorno!
Good evening! = Buona Sera!
Good night! = Buona Notte!
Goodbye! = Arrivederci!

OTHER IMPORTANT SENTENCES

My name is ... = Mi chiamo ...
I am German/ I am German = Sono tedesca/ Sono tedesco
How much does it cost? = Quanto costa?
Where is the train station? = Dov è la stazione?
Where is the post office? = Dov è l ufficio postale?
Where is the airport? = Dov è l aeroporto?
I need a doctor = Ho bisogno di un dottore

Closing words

This book is slowly coming to an end. I hope that you have gained many useful and informative tips while reading it and that you have become enthusiastic about Rome.

In the first chapter, I asked you, dear reader, what you associate with the Eternal City and what Rome means to you. Perhaps you were initially particularly impressed or attracted by just one facet of this city. Perhaps you already knew a little about Rome from stories told by other travelers. But even if the city was completely unknown and new to you, I hope that you will all say after your stay there: 'Rome. This is the city that is always worth a visit!

In the best case scenario, even the history buffs among you will now also become enthusiastic art connoisseurs and they in turn will discover modern treasures for themselves on a shopping trip through Rome. How nice would it be if you had originally set out on your trip to Rome with a spiritual motivation and then also kept many secular experiences of your trip in good memory or if you were stranded in Rome at some point completely unbiased and rather by chance and then fell head over heels in love with the city?

One thing would be certain: this love would last forever! But I am also sure that you will see and experience so much in this beautiful city that you could write entire books about it afterwards.

So, whatever takes you to Rome one day, I very much hope that your trip will be an unforgettable experience that you will remember fondly for a long time to come and that you will be able to say to yourself at the end:

Ti amo, Roma!